Dedicated to the wonder in each of us.

Moments of Wonder

LIFE WITH MORITZ

Barry J. Schieber

Illustrations by Kelynn Z. Alder

SILENT MOON BOOKS

SILENT MOON BOOKS

Post Office Box 1865
Bigfork, Montana 59911
www.silentmoonbooks.com
E-MAIL info@silentmoonbooks.com

ISBN 978-0-9721457-4-9
All Rights Reserved

Copyright 2008
Silent Moon Books

Illustrations Copyright 2008
by Kelynn Z. Alder

Cover photo: www.thomasrogowski.ch

Printed in China

Contents

Acknowledgments

Moritz's and my life has been immeasurably enriched by the kindness of friends and strangers.

I wish to express my gratitude.

It is customary to list friends who have been especially helpful. This time I wish to thank them in person and acknowledge those unexpected people who extend themselves to help us and then continue on their way.

Often our meetings are brief—barely long enough to say thank you. Someone will carry our bags, walk us to the bus, invite us to their home to stay when we travel, help us to visit schools and libraries, show us their favorite hiking trails—in short, care for us.

Thank you, too, to the international airline personnel, who shepherd Moritz through transatlantic flights: pilots, stewardesses and stewards, and most often the porters who take Moritz in his kennel to the airplane. So many times I have looked into the eyes of porters who, seeing Moritz, graciously accept the responsibility of taking care of him.

Of course, my gratitude overflows for Moritz. His gentle, calm, noble nature and his innate awareness constantly remind me of the power of benevolence. Throughout the world, people respond to him with generosity and happiness.

It is something to behold.

Every Day is Today...

Introduction

Moritz trained as a therapy dog.

His visits to patients in the hospital are chronicled in *Nose to Nose: A Memoir of Healing*. But it seems that Moritz had contributions to make in other settings as well. His first book written expressly for children, *A Gift to Share: The Story of Moritz*, opened the door to visits to schools and libraries, where he also seemed to help people, especially children with special needs. Two more children's books, *An Open Heart: A Story About Moritz* and *A Peaceful Mind: Travels with Moritz*, show him as an ambassador of good will.

Day in, day out, life with Moritz has strung together many moments of wonder. With Moritz, every day is today—not tomorrow, not yesterday, just today. Perhaps you will glimpse this wonder in the stories that follow.

Today...

Once again I jump into the back of the car, resting beside two backpacks. Barry's friend Peggy has joined us for a hike in the Jewel Basin Wilderness. I know the way up the road to the trailhead, and as soon as we go off the pavement onto the gravel road, I jump up and look out the window. Barry lowers the glass so I can smell all the fragrances of the forest.

It's a hot day; the road is dry and dusty.

We park the car and begin the hike to the top of Mount Aeneas. Near the beginning of the trail, there's a small creek that's nearly dry. Barry says, "Drink, Moritz. Have some water. The trail may be dry, so drink now." But I'm too excited to drink and run up the trail, looking back to see if Peggy and Barry understand that it's time to get moving.

As we climb the trail, I feel hotter and hotter. Every so often I find some shade and lie down to catch my breath. When we reach the top of the mountain, we find a place to rest and have a snack. I go to a shady place to sit, looking across the valley to the peaks of Glacier Park. Several small turquoise lakes shimmer below us in the summer sun. On a day like today, Jewel Basin sure lives up to its name. Rested, we head back down the mountain.

It was cool on the top of the mountain, but I am getting warmer as we go lower into the valley. I tire easily on these hot summer afternoons; my black fur is thick and warm and soaks up the heat. I am much more comfortable in the ice and snow.

Usually, we stop at a lake or river so I can drink and take a cool dip, but there is no water along the trail. By now, I'm hot again.

After a few miles we stop. Peggy pulls her water bottle from her backpack and takes a long drink. She looks at me. My tongue is hanging out and I am panting.

"Moritz!" she exclaims. "You need some water."

She kneels next to me and cups her hands. "Barry, pour some water in my hands," she commands. Barry carefully pours out some water. First I sniff it; then I begin drinking, slowly at first, then quickly, so that Barry has to keep refilling Peggy's hands. This is a new experience for me—with my big tongue it's hard to lap the water, and I spill most of it on Peggy, but it's a lot of fun. When I finish, I smack my lips. Peggy puts her cool, wet hands on my head. Boy, do they feel good! I step back for a moment and look at Peggy; then I walk toward her, briefly staring into her eyes. I want to thank her, so I plant a big slurpy kiss on both her cheeks.

Peggy is surprised. My sudden gesture of affection has touched her. She's not quite sure what to say.

She whispers, "Oh, Moritz." 🐾

Today...

We are up before sunrise. I love this time of day. The air is fresh, and there are stars are in the sky. I begin to bark and run in circles around Barry.

Barry shouts, "Moritz, stop barking and get in the car. We're going to Whitefish for our yoga class. You're going to see all your friends. Now hush."

I jump in the car. Barry gives me a treat, and I lie down.

Every Sunday we drive to a yoga studio where Barry teaches Kum Nye, Tibetan Relaxation. Through slow movement and meditation, the exercises balance the body and mind. There are a lot of Kum Nye students in Whitefish.

I leap from the car to greet the students who are gathered outside, waiting for Barry to unlock the studio door. A chorus of warm greetings echoes down the street. "Hello, Moritz." "Come say hello." "How are you?" Such a welcome. I greet everyone with my tail wagging, muscle my way between legs, and check to see if anyone has brought me a biscuit.

Barry opens the door and we climb the stairs to the yoga room. All the students take off their shoes before they step onto the shiny yellow wood floor. Everyone takes a mat and a meditation cushion from the closet and finds a place to practice. I follow Barry to his mat. I face the students, slide my front legs forward, bow down in a

long stretch, loosening my back, and yawn. Then I lie down next to him. This morning a new couple has joined the class.

Barry introduces himself and asks, "Does anyone mind if Moritz joins us?"

No one minds.

He welcomes the new students and asks them to introduce themselves. Their names are Bev and Al; they are here on vacation. As Bev talks, her eyes are on me. Barry notices this and says, "Moritz is a therapy dog. He is a regular member of our class."

Bev smiles, but she looks sad.

Class begins, and I roll over on my side to nap.

The exercises are gentle and slow moving, and following each set is a period of meditation. Often after meditation Barry will ask a few questions.

Directly across from us, Andrea is looking uncomfortable. Barry asks, "What are you feeling?"

Andrea begins to cry. She says, "My right arm feels like a broken chicken wing." As she sits there, the tears roll down her cheeks, and soon she is sobbing.

I open my eyes to see who is crying. I stand up, shake myself, and slowly walk across the room to Andrea. When I am right in front of her, I stretch again, in what I have been told is the "downward-facing dog" yoga pose. Andrea lifts her face, and I look directly into her eyes. The room is completely quiet as we share this moment.

Andrea reaches out and pulls me closer. She hugs me and holds me before letting me go. I walk over to Bev and Al. I stop in front of each of them, and they hug and pet me. Then I go back and lie down by Barry.

Quietly we sit, and again Barry asks Andrea, "What are you feeling?"

"This morning I felt tense, tight, walled in, as if I were encased in a shell. My breathing was shallow and uneven, and I felt heavy. My arm has been a problem, but today it just wouldn't work, and I felt frustrated, weak, and disconnected. But as I lifted my head to look at Moritz, suddenly I saw him as a kind and wise companion. And suddenly my body released all the tension, and I feel refreshed in every cell, and grateful."

The room is silent once again.

Barry says, "These relaxation exercises may be simple to do, but they are powerful. They can release inner energy blocks."

He looks at Bev and asks,

"Do you have something you wish to add?"

Bev doesn't hesitate.

"I am so touched to see Moritz react to her pain. Just to see him stare lovingly into her eyes brought tears to mine. Then to stop and say hello to Al and me before he went back to you. He must have sensed how much we're still missing our dog who passed away a month ago." 🐾

Today...

Lou Anne Krantz greets us with a warm smile. Lou Anne is the librarian at Polson Middle School, in Polson, Montana. She has invited Barry and me to speak to the children. And now here we are, about to be guests at an assembly of the entire school.

Walking to the library, Lou Anne tells Barry, "The children think your books are special because they're true stories about a real dog. All the children have read the books or heard them read aloud. So they are excited about meeting Moritz, and you."

We go into the library. Its door wears a colorful poster the children made to welcome us. Inside, a crowd of children are waiting in line to drop books off on a table. In exchange for the books, each child is handed a coupon. I can see that this school has prepared for our visit, because everyone knows my name and asks politely if it's OK to pet me.

Lou Anne tells us that the books are for children in Papua New Guinea. She says that not long ago, a man from Habitat for Humanity called her. He said that the children there didn't have any books. The man asked her if she could find some used books for these children. That gave her an idea. She would ask her students to bring in old books. In return for each donation, she would give the student a coupon good for buying *Nose to Nose* at a discount. Students could also write letters explaining "Why I would like a copy of *Nose to Nose*." A committee of teachers would choose the ten best letters, and the children who wrote them would each win a free book, pawprinted by me and autographed by Barry. After the assembly, we are going to sit in the library and meet the winners.

"Moritz," says Barry, "we better be on our toes this morning. Everyone here has read about you and has questions for us."

We walk into the school gym. The bleachers are filled, and the kids spot me. They start to applaud. "Moritz!" they shout. "Moritz!"

Calmly I walk beside Barry, off leash, to center court. Barry stops and I slowly stretch and lie down. As I do so, the noise grows much louder.

When at last the gym is quiet, Barry introduces me. He tells the children that I am a Bernese mountain dog. He tells them that I am a certified therapy dog who goes to hospitals and visits patients. He tells them that I weigh 115 pounds, and that I am eight years old. He tells them how we met in Switzerland, and that we now live in Montana. He even tells them how much I eat.

Barry says he will read them a story from *Nose to Nose*, the one about Cody, a boy we visited in the hospital. Cody was ten years old. Barry asks how many of them are ten. A lot of hands shoot up. Barry promises that after he reads them the story, they can ask as many questions as they like.

The gym is still. Everyone is listening to Barry but staring at me.

As soon as Barry finishes reading, he is swamped with questions.

"Does he like to hike?" "Can he do tricks?" "Where does he sleep?" Then Barry turns the tables and asks them questions. "How many of you have dogs?" (Almost all of them do; after all, this is Montana.) "Have you ever seen a dog in the hospital?" "Is anyone afraid of dogs?"

The questions and answers continue, interrupted by bursts of laughter, until our assembly time ends. Now Lou Anne takes us to the library. I lie down under the table, and Barry takes out my paw-print stamp. The children who wrote the winning letters line up to receive their books. As they wait, they come over to pet me and ask more questions. Barry speaks to each child while he stamps and signs their book. He asks them if someday they might want to write a book of their own.

When we finish, Barry asks Lou Anne how many books the students donated for the children of Papua New Guinea. She says, "I'm not sure exactly, but I think over a thousand." Barry's eyes open wide, and he lets out a soft, low whistle. I know that means he's surprised, and probably impressed.

Here is one of the winning letters:

Dear Moritz and Barry,

There are lots of reasons I would absolutely love to have the book _Nose To Nose_. Mrs. Kranz read our reading class about Moritz making a very old woman in a wheel chair happy. That story was heart warming, so reading a whole bunch of stories like that would make me feel great.

Another reason I would like to win this heart warming book would be for my Grandma because my grandfather just died and my grandma is having a real rough time by herself. She loves animals. She has 14 cats, 4 dogs and a lot of cows. So I would give it to her to give her a happy moment.

And if I got it I would be able to get it signed and that would be such a wonderful experience and my grandma would probably like it even more if it was sighed.

Today...

We're going to visit a teenage girl who must go to court. In a few weeks she will be a witness in a trial. If she likes me, and if her family agrees, I will sit beside her when she takes the witness stand. Maybe I can help her stay calm while she testifies.

As we pull up to her home, I see my friend Bea, the psychologist. Bea is going to introduce us to the family. We walk through the front door into a commotion—two babies crying, three children sitting on the couch watching TV, toys scattered all over, and three dogs yapping in the backyard. I feel the tension in the room. On the couch I see a teenage girl looking nervously at me. She sits up and calls, "Moritz." I walk over to her and lie down on the floor, with my hind end on her feet. She giggles and reaches down to pet me. Bea introduces Mary. I'm quiet, and for a few seconds all the commotion stops. Then the children run over to pet, poke, and play with me.

Softly, Mary asks Bea what it will be like to go to court. While they talk about what it might be like, I lie quietly at Mary's feet.

Before we leave, Bea asks Mary, "Would you like Moritz to sit beside you while you are on the witness stand?"

Mary hesitates for a few moments. Shyly she says, "I think so, if my parents say it's OK."

"Think it over," Bea tells her. "We'll meet again in a few weeks and you can let me know what you decide."

When we meet again, Mary runs up to hug me and tells Bea her parents have said yes.

Bea asks, "How do you feel about Moritz?"

She replies, "He's soooo soothing."

Bea says, "Good; we're all set. We'll meet at the courthouse next Monday morning at ten."

But that doesn't happen. The case is rescheduled, and it's another three months before Barry and I go to the county courthouse.

Barry stops before we go in and bends over to tell me, "Moritz, today you will sit beside Mary on the witness stand. You're the first dog in the county to be able to do that. If all goes well, people will see how much you help. It wasn't that long ago that hospitals wouldn't allow dogs to visit patients. Perhaps the courts will be next."

We enter the courthouse. No one stops us. No one asks us what I am doing there. We get on an elevator and get off in a waiting room outside the courtroom. This room reminds me of many of the hospitals we have visited. It smells like disinfectant, and it has cold floors and rows of chairs. I am curious to look around, but Barry holds the leash tightly. I walk quietly beside him through a small crowd of people who are sitting around and talking. As we pass, they look up, and a tense hush fills the room. Barry finds a seat in the corner where we won't disturb anyone and tells me to lie down.

For a few minutes the room is quiet. Then one by one, people come over to say hello and pet me. They giggle, gasp, laugh, and ask the usual questions. "What's his name?" "It's a boy, right?" "How much does he weigh?" "Does he eat a lot?" "How old is he?"

The tension has left the room and everyone seems more relaxed.

We wait to see what we are supposed to do. Bea appears and comes over to tell us we can take a lunch break while the jury is being chosen.

An hour later, the jury still hasn't been chosen, and we are told to wait in a room on the second floor, where people who might be chosen as jurors won't see me. The judge and both sets of attorneys knew that I was coming, but now that the defendant's attorneys have seen me, and they don't want me to be on the witness stand with Mary. They don't even want the jury to see me. They say I would be a distraction.

We wait on the second floor. As we sit, attorneys, policemen, and policewomen come over to visit. One policeman exclaims, "What a wonderful dog!" A social worker drops to her knees to play with me. She tells us she understands how helpful I could be and is doing her best to get us admitted to the courtroom. People in the courthouse seem to have a lot on their minds. Just like the doctors and nurses in the hospital, they rush out of the elevator, charging ahead in a swirl of purpose. Then they see me lying with my head between my paws. Suddenly they stop, turn around, and come over to greet me, say a few words, and take a breath. I like how natural this feels.

At 3 pm the trial will begin. Mary will be the first witness. We can't go into the courtroom even to watch. We have to wait until we are called. While we are waiting, a county attorney comes over to pet me. She begins telling us stories about her dogs. She knows I am a therapy dog. She says, "I think he could help the children to relax on the witness stand. I hope to start a program that allows dogs in the courtroom. Good luck. I wish you success."

At 4:45 pm Bea comes to tell us that the case has recessed for the day. Mary wasn't called. We'll come back tomorrow morning, when Mary takes the stand.

Just before she leaves, Bea turns and says, "There's a buzz about how well behaved and gentle Moritz is. He has already made quite an impression."

The next morning when we get off the elevator, people stop us to say hello. An elderly man, perhaps Mary's grandfather, asks if anyone has given me a gift. He says the family wants to give me a bone and asks if anyone has delivered it to Moritz. Barry says, "No, not yet; we just arrived."

Everyone else is called into the courtroom. We go to the second floor to wait. After two hours, Bea comes to get us. She says the judge decided not to allow me in the courtroom. The only reason he gave was that the defense attorneys objected. The ruling was a surprise, and Bea is disappointed. Finally she takes us to a small conference room.

Mary is sitting at a table with her head resting on her arms. She sees me and sits up. I go to greet her. I lie down, and she sits on the floor to hug me. She backs up until she is under the table and calls my name. I scoot next to her and she nestles close. She has been testifying all morning, and the court is now on a break.

After half an hour, Bea tells Mary it's time to go back and finish her testimony.

Mary crawls out from under the table. With a bit more energy in her voice, she says, "OK. Let's go."

Barry says, "Mary, we'll see you later. Moritz and I are going home now. Let us know how it goes."

That evening Bea phones to tell us that Mary did really well. After the break, she seemed more confident, less afraid.

Barry calls me to come and sit by him. He hugs me, pulls a treat from his pocket, and gives it to me.

"Moritz," he says, "even though you weren't allowed in the courtroom, you helped Mary, and you made a big impression on the people who count. Soon, thanks to you, there may be a program to allow dogs in Montana courtrooms." 🐾

Today...

We are walking along the canals in Amsterdam on a windy day. I've learned that in this city I have to be really alert. Bicycles are everywhere—on roads, bike paths, sidewalks, and crowding the intersections.

And they carry everything—plants, boxes, children, and groceries, with people behind the seat and on the handlebars. Yet the traffic flows smoothly and everybody is friendly.

It took me awhile to learn to pay attention to the bikes. Now, when I hear the bike bell's ring-a-ling, it reminds me to be aware and get out of the way.

Barry usually speaks to me before we go across the street. "Moritz," he says, "Come." This alerts me that we will cross the street and I need to pay extra attention.

I look up and follow Barry to a pharmacy. Behind the counter, a man has just finished waiting on a customer. As he greets us, he stops and stares.

"What kind of dog is that?" he asks Barry.

"A Bernese mountain dog."

"His name?"

"Moritz."

A moment goes by.

"Can I take his picture?"

"Sure."

I watch while he takes out his cell phone to snap a picture of me, and then pauses.

"Would you wait a moment? I would like to call my partner."

"Sure."

He turns, opens the curtain to the back room, and calls, "Could you come out? I want you to see someone."

A friendly looking man appears. He looks at me, staring intensely.

"Hello," he says to Barry. "I am from the Philippines, and when I grew up we had two cats. Each morning our family would go to our meditation room to pray. The cats had their own place and always prayed with us. No matter where they were in the house, when we went to pray they scampered to their place. There is something about your dog that reminds me."

He continues to stare at me.

Barry asks, "Could you describe what it is you see? What is it that connects you with Moritz?"

I watch as a tear rolls down the man's cheek and he begins to cry. In a low voice he replies, "Perhaps his calm, his sense of peace." 🐾

Today...

We have been visiting patients in the hospital. Katie, our hosptial rehabilitation aide, is with us. As we walk down the hall of the rehab unit, around the corner swings an elderly woman slumped in a wheel-chair, accompanied by two physical therapists. Above her shoulder an IV bottle hangs on a hook, and a tube runs down her side to the back of her hand.

We see each other at the same moment.

"Come!" she calls, and I trot to her side. She throws her left arm around me and hugs me, pulling me closer. I lay my head against her chest, and she runs her IV-bandaged arm affectionately up and down my back.

Barry kneels down to look into her face. "Lady," he says, "you're brave to grab such a big dog without the slightest hesitation."

She laughs loudly. "I've had dogs all my life. I love them!" With everyone laughing, I return to Barry and sit by his side. The woman looks at me with sparkling eyes and softly says,

"Thanks, big boy."

One of the therapists whispers something to Katie.

As we part company, Katie asks, "Did you hear what the therapist said?"

"No."

"That patient's stroke left her with left hemiplegia and left neglect. That means that she doesn't know that she has the left side of her body. Her reaction, the spontaneous use of her left arm, was completely unexpected. She hasn't been able to move it for the past six months." 🐾

Today...

The Special Olympics Montana Committee has invited us to the Big Mountain Ski Resort in Whitefish. Children with mental disabilities from all over the state compete in ski and snowshoe races for gold medals.

This year each medal winner will have his or her photo taken on the slopes with me. It seems people have been told that I am a famous Swiss rescue dog. Let me correct this notion. I haven't been trained, like some Bernese, to do mountain rescue work, helping to find people who have been lost or hurt. Barry has told me how dedicated, brave, and smart those dogs are. He thinks I would be good at this work too, because I am fearless and strong and love the snowy mountains. But really, I am a therapy dog. I go to hospitals to visit patients. Some of them have been rescued from accidents and brought to the hospital to heal.

The sky is overcast, and it's cold. The mountainside is crowded with racers, their families and friends, and other people who have come to watch. We stand where we are told, not far from the finish line and the awards podium.

Kathy Sullivan, a local photographer, has volunteered to take a picture of each winner and me. But the children are not quite sure where to go, or how to approach me. Often, when they see how big I am, they hesitate.

Gently Kathy guides them toward me and tells me to sit. I sit, and the first winner, all smiles, comes close and hugs me. Seeing that I'm friendly, some even hang their medals around my neck. It doesn't take long for the word to spread. Soon kids are asking if the photos can be made into posters so they can hang them in their bedrooms.

Barry said we would be on the mountain for an hour or two. But it's been four hours, and the line for photos is still growing. As I look up the slope, I see kids laughing and playing in a long, long line that disappears around the side of the mountain.

Every hour Barry calls a break and takes me to walk and play in the snow. Thank goodness! I slide down the hillside, dig in the snowbanks, roll over and over and chew mouthfuls of snow. It's heaven!

Then it's back for more photos. We remain on the mountain all afternoon.

It's getting dark when Karen Kimball, our Olympic host, comes over to me and says, "OK, Moritz, you can go home. Thank you for your patience and for the joy you have brought all of us." 🐾

Today...

We get up before dawn. Barry rushes about, dressing, making tea, showering, and packing his backpack. I feel his energy and know we are about to leave for a trip. Excited, I follow him around the house to let him know that I am ready and that I plan to go along.

"Moritz!" Barry shouts, "Go lie down! Of course you are coming. Please lie down." Reluctantly, I go to my bed, but I keep a close eye on him.

"Let's go, Mo," he calls. "We're ready to go to Spokane."

As we drive up our road to the highway, Barry explains why we are going to Spokane, Washington, which is hours away.

"Moritz, last week I heard from a woman whose neighbor's little girl has leukemia. The little girl has read *Nose to Nose* and has fallen in love with you. All she does is talk about you and about how she's going to have a Bernese some day and train it to become a therapy dog. The little girl's name is Bella. She is now in the hospital in Spokane. She'll be there for eight weeks, and her friend has asked us to visit her. I spoke with Bella's parents, and they said yes. So today we are going to the hospital to surprise Bella.

"Now you know why I bathed and brushed you yesterday. You need to look mighty handsome today."

It is snowing when we arrive in Spokane. The Sacred Heart Children's Hospital sits on a hill overlooking the city. In morning light, with snow falling, it reminds me of a Swiss castle.

Outside the hospital, Barry takes me for a brief walk. He knows I love the cold. I breathe in the brisk air, stretch and roll over in the snow.

Then Barry wipes the snow off me, and we go into the hospital. We take the elevator up to the Oncology unit. When the elevator doors open, we walk into a sparkling clean corridor filled with pastel colors—pink, yellow, and blue. Two women smile at us. One looks at me and asks,

"Who is this?"

"This is Moritz. He is here to visit Bella and her family."

"Oh my! Tell me more."

"You can see for yourself. But I have some books in my backpack if you would like to read about him." Barry, the ever-ready salesman, pulls out a copy of *Nose to Nose* and hands it to her.

She looks it over, and exclaims, "Everyone should have this book!"

Barry seems surprised, but he agrees and asks, "Who are you?"

"I'm Karen. I'm the parent and patient advocate. Can I buy two books? Oh, I'm sorry, but I don't have any money with me."

Barry hands her a business card and tells her to send the money later.

Now she is surprised. "You trust me?"

Barry laughs. "Of course. You look trustworthy."

We begin to walk down the hallway toward four people who are looking at us.

"You must be Moritz and Barry?"

"Yes."

"We're Bella's Mom and Dad and these are our boys. We're happy to meet you."

All eyes are on me. But no one comes to greet me, so I approach them, tail wagging, to say hello. This breaks the ice and both boys quickly begin to pet me.

Barry asks, "Is Moritz bigger than you imagined?"

"Oh, yes!" they agree. "Way bigger."

Bella's Dad leads us into her room. Bella is lying down. A tube runs from her chest to a monitor. Her skin is yellow.

Her mother says, "Bella, look. Moritz has come to visit you."

Bella moves slowly to sit up. She sees me and looks puzzled.

Her mother says, "Yes, this is Moritz, the dog you read about. Dad and I thought you would like to meet him. So we asked Barry to bring him here. Do you want to pet him?"

Bella hesitates. I approach her bed and look into her eyes. She reaches out to touch my head. Then she sits up and focuses on me. I lie down by her bed. Her brothers come over to play with me.

Her Mom says, "Would you like to get down on the floor with him?" Bella nods yes.

Her mother helps her to the floor, careful not to disturb the tubes or monitor, and Bella rests her head on my back. After a few moments she sits up and gently pets me, head to tail. Barry has brought a copy of each of our books for Bella. He flips through to show her some of his favorite illustrations.

While Bella is looking through a book, Barry pulls out a stuffed Bernese mountain dog toy. It looks like a small version of me. Bella's eyes open wide, but she remains quiet on the floor with me.

Bella's mother has been closely watching me. She says softly, "He's so calm."

Barry says, "Yes, he's calm. He's been calm ever since he was a puppy. He's not trained to be calm. It's just Moritz."

"How did you know to bring him to hospitals? How did you know he would make a good therapy dog?"

"Do you think he was made to sit in a backyard? Moritz has so much to offer."

"Of course. He has such presence." Bella's mother whispers, "There are no words to describe how I feel."

She begins to cry as she thanks us for coming to visit Bella. 🐾

Today...

Barry and I have been going to a lot of schools lately to meet with children, teachers, and sometimes parents. This morning we arrive at an elementary school, Barry takes off my leash and I poke my nose into offices and classrooms, creating quite a stir. Children giggle, shout and point their fingers at me. School secretaries, teachers, and even the principal stop their work to come greet me. Oh boy, I stir up a whole lot of excitement!

With all the noise, it's not long before a teacher comes to lead us to the library. As we walk down the hall, I put my head in every classroom. I am curious to see what's inside. Sometimes I see turtles, guinea pigs, hamsters, parrots, but always I see smiling faces.

At the end of the hall is the library. It's a beautiful room, filled with light. A hundred or so children are sitting on the floor waiting for us. It's time to get to work.

I trot right over to a little boy and sniff him as he looks into my eyes and pets me. Leaving him, I circle around the children. I see the teachers on their folding chairs, carefully keeping one eye on the kids and the other eye on me. They don't quite know what to make of me.

I walk over to one teacher. She looks at me, notices how big I am (I am pretty big), and leans back ever so slightly, trying to put a bit more space between us. She gently pats my head, as if to reassure me, and herself, that all is well.

I return her greeting by sniffing around her right knee. My nose moves down her leg, and I spend awhile exploring her right ankle, sniffing, smelling, and licking once or twice.

Suddenly, she bursts into tears. In seconds, her cheeks are wet and she is sobbing. Just then Barry calls me to the front of the room to join him for our presentation. As usual, he talks about us and our adventures together and reads from one of our books. Once he begins, I lie down by his side.

After the talk, the children pepper Barry with questions. He answers them all, sometimes gently, sometimes with a bit of challenge. As they file out of the library, the teacher, her cheeks still moist, comes over and introduces herself.

"My name is Sandy Johnson, and I want you to know these are tears of joy."

"Tears of joy?" Barry asks.

"Yes. Moritz knows."

"He knows?"

"Yes. My right foot has been operated on three times in the past year, and when school is out next month I will go to Seattle for another operation. This is my last chance to see if my foot can be saved."

Her voice shakes a little and she looks frightened.

"Somehow I feel Moritz is aware of my pain and fear. I felt he was trying gently to reassure me that my foot will be saved, and I will be fine.

"He seems so sure of himself. He didn't hesitate to check me out with that sensitive nose."

Barry says, "Thank you for explaining. I wasn't sure what happened between you and Moritz, and I'm thrilled that you found Moritz so comforting. May we come visit you after the operation?"

Sandy smiles and says, "Please do."

Late in the summer, Barry and I go to visit Sandy. I prance into her house, spot her in a wheelchair, put my head briefly in her lap, and then set off to explore the house. I hear Barry explain to Sandy that when I put my head in her lap, I was sending her my "not to worry" message. When I come back from checking out the kitchen, Sandy looks a lot more relaxed.

A few days later, Barry tells me that Sandy phoned to say that after our visit she stopped worrying. At her checkup she learned that her foot had been saved. She felt her two visits with me had made all the difference. Setting worry aside had helped her to heal. 🐾

Today...

Sunday mornings in Amsterdam are quiet. We leave our room early in the morning, heading to the bakery for fresh bread. In the early morning sunlight, the city glows. We walk slowly through the maze of canals, over bridges and through neighborhood parks. Sometimes I go first, sometimes Barry does. We are in no hurry, just enjoying ourselves.

We come to a big street full of cars. I sit by Barry's side and wait for his command to cross.

Suddenly, we hear a woman shouting, "I can't believe it!"

Across the street I see a pretty woman in a jogging suit and a Boston Red Sox cap, waving her arms and calling us. We cross the street. Even before we reach the curb, questions come tumbling toward us.

"Hello, hello, can I take your picture? I mean, can I take a picture of your dog? What's his name? What breed? Where did you get him? Where do you live? Maybe you could take a picture of the two of us? Wait until I tell my husband!"

As she pauses for breath, Barry calmly replies, "Sure, you can take your pictures. How come you're so excited?"

"Yesterday my husband and I saw your dog for just a moment, before you disappeared behind a bus. Last night we were talking about our three favorite images of Amsterdam. Your dog was one of them!"

Barry takes a deep breath and says, "What do you do for a living?"

"I'm a sports reporter. My name is Lesley Visser. My husband is Dick Stockton." Barry recognizes Dick's name and says,

"Tell Dick I enjoy his basketball broadcasts. He has a fan club of at least one in Montana."

Lesley nods, but she isn't really listening. She is upset because her camera isn't working. She tries again and again to take our picture. No luck. Frustrated, she asks if we will come to the Amstel Hotel to meet Dick. "He won't believe it!"

She is so enthusiastic and charming that it's hard for Barry to say no. He looks at me and asks, "What do you think, Moritz? Would you like to see a beautiful hotel and meet Dick?"

I know he's trying to slow Lesley down and get her to stop asking so many questions. Besides, he knows I am ready to go—anywhere.

On our walk to the hotel, Lesley continues questioning Barry.

"Did you really write a book about Moritz? What is it about? Where do I get one? Why did you write the book? What are you doing in Amsterdam?"

We reach the Amstel, an elegant old five-star hotel with a long entrance staircase covered in red carpet. We climb the stairs, but before we can enter the lobby, the doorman stops us.

"Sorry, we do not allow dogs in the hotel," he says.

Lesley is busy trying to get her camera to work. Barry and I sit on the stairs to wait. A bellhop comes over to say, "Good-looking dog" and Lesley instantly wails that her camera is broken. He offers to get her a new one and disappears into the hotel. Moments later he returns with a new camera.

Lesley thanks him, shoots a dozen photos of me, and then goes inside to tell Dick to come down immediately. She does not tell him why. Lesley must like surprises.

As we wait, people arrive at the hotel and come over to pet me.

"Dick's coming," Lesley shouts. "You and Moritz go sit on the bottom stair."

Dick is an athletic-looking man, dressed in a jogging suit. His hair is a bit ruffled, as if he had been asleep. Lesley points to me and squeals, "Look!"

I see Dick glance over Barry and spot me.

"Wow!" he hollers.

He races down the stairs to greet me. Before he touches me, he looks at Barry, who says,

"He's friendly."

Dick falls to his knees and begins petting me. He begins asking questions, just like Lesley.

"Where are you from? Did you follow baseball as a boy? Who were your favorite teams? Did you ever go to the World Series?" He fires questions steadily at Barry, not pausing for breath, while he rolls me over and rubs my belly and scratches my ears.

After a few moments and dozens of questions, Barry raises his hand and says with a laugh,

"Lesley has already done the interview. She'll fill you in. However, I have a question for you. What is it about this dog that has you so enthralled? What has you playing here with Moritz on a Sunday morning, as if the two of you were old friends?"

Dick stops and sits up. He looks as if he is repeating the question to himself, silently wondering: What is it? He looks at me. I lie with my head between my paws, my eyes on him.

He turns to Lesley, who sits on the stairs, awaiting his answer.

Another moment passes, and quietly Dick answers,

"I want to be like him." 🐾

Today...

My friends Pooh and Ginny have come to hike to Morrell Falls in the Seeley-Swan mountain range. Pooh is a handsome golden retriever/chow mix with a thick red-orange fur, floppy ears, and a white muzzle. Fourteen years old, he walks slowly, but he's still the most adventurous dog I know. He constantly goes off the trail, often in chase of squirrels. He's like a mischievous cousin who comes to visit.

Ginny is a fit, outdoors-loving Montana woman who is a perfect companion for him. She's patient, watchful, tolerant, and so sweet. Whenever they visit, we have a good time together.

It is a beautiful July morning, a bit cool, sunny, birds, and chipmunks chirping, and best of all only the four of us are hiking this trail. Barry is trying to talk to Ginny, but he has to keep turning around, stopping to wait for them to catch up. I run back to them, then ahead, practicing my herding skills. Barry is practicing his patience. Pooh is sniffing under every log and up every tree. Occasionally, he pokes his nose down some hole in the rocks. He must have been lively when he was younger. Now his legs are old and he walks slowly.

The trail climbs gradually to the falls. After awhile, we find a pace that lets Ginny and Barry talk while we dogs sniff around on our own. Occasionally Ginny or Barry calls us and I return, but Pooh just keeps moving through the brush, too busy to pay attention.

Near the falls is little Morrell Lake, off the trail and surrounded by a swampy shoreline.

Suddenly, Ginny realizes that Pooh has disappeared. "Oh, Pooh!" she shouts, "Come!" She calls him over and over. But Pooh has vanished. Ginny looks anxious. Barry says, "He must be off in the brush. You go back along the trail. I'll go ahead, and we'll keep calling him."

I can't decide whether to go with Barry or with Ginny. I decide to go with Ginny. After a few minutes we meet up where we parted. Pooh is still missing. Ginny says, "Moritz, please go find Pooh."

I look at Ginny. She looks really scared. I lift my nose toward the sky, trying to pick up Pooh's scent. I sniff, sniff again, and sniff once more. Then I push through the brush to the lake and take Ginny to Pooh. He's up to his neck in a marsh. His head is covered with mud. Even his nose is muddy. At some point, his head must have gone completely under!

Ginny wades into the muck, grabs Pooh by the scruff of his neck, and yanks him up. Using all her strength, she pulls him onto solid ground, covered in mud from his ears to his tail. She seems shaken but relieved. Pooh, calm as ever, gives her his usual look—a look that says, "You worry too much. Everything's fine." All the same, he seems glad to be out.

Barry is waiting on the trail, and I go back to his side. Ginny and Pooh come out of the brush, and Barry bursts out laughing at the sight of my two mud-coated friends.

Ginny laughs too and asks, "How far to the falls? We both need a shower."

It is not far. Ginny leads Pooh straight under the waterfall. At first he moves away, as though he's not too sure that this is a good idea. But Ginny sits him on a rock and begins to scrub him, crooning, "You Old Pooh! Really, you have made quite the mess." And Pooh suddenly relaxes and lies in the shallow water to help her get him clean. Finally, the two of them walk out from under the waterfall. Pooh shakes to dry off, and they return to us.

Barry calls, "Hi, Pooh. Having fun?"

Ginny turns to me. For a moment, she doesn't say anything.

She just looks. Then she hugs me and says, "Moritz. Thank you. Forever." 🐾

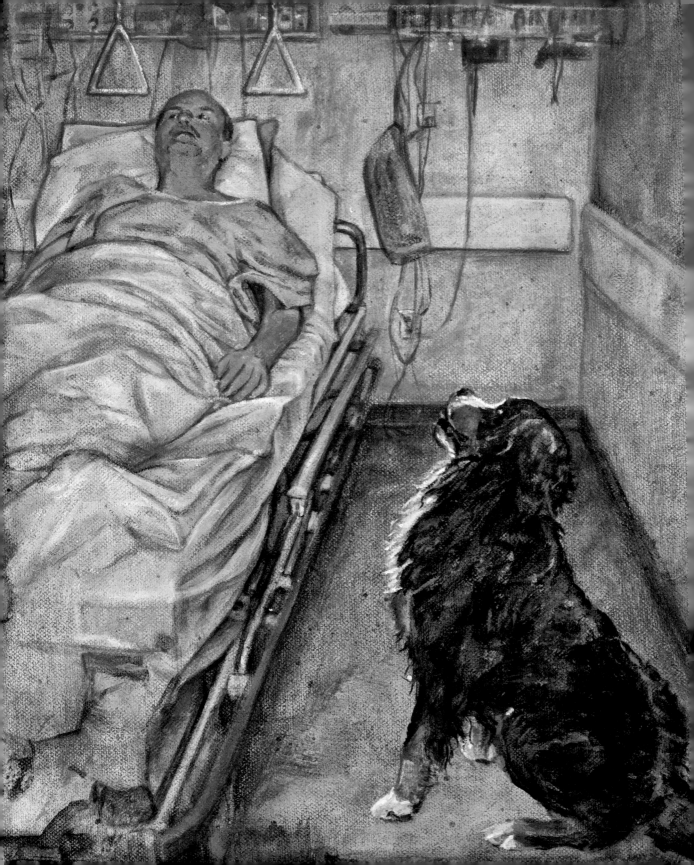

Today...

We are visiting Community Medical Center, a hospital in Missoula, Montana, where Barry and I voluteer as a pet therapy team. This is my weekly work, and I enjoy visiting all the patients, young and old.

I know nearly everyone who works in the hospital, including the doctors, nurses, housekeepers, and the people who work in the offices. They're always glad to see me; often they have homemade treats for me.

We enter a dimly lit room, bare of flowers and cards. Katie, the rehabilitation aide who ushers us around the hospital, is with us. In the back of the room, a middle-aged man lies staring at two triangle grips suspended from the ceiling. His breath is short and shallow.

"Good morning, Jim. Would you like to see a beautiful therapy dog? He's big enough to reach your bed," Katie calls.

Jim remains tense and motionless, barely turning his head to see who is talking to him. I start to walk toward him. Then I suddenly back away and lie down on the floor. Katie looks surprised. Usually I walk directly to the patient and touch his arm or hand or get close enough so that I can be petted. This time I lie with my head between my paws a few feet away from the bed.

Katie says, "Could Moritz get closer to Jim?"

"Moritz," Barry says, "Stand. Come on, Moritz, get up and say hello to Jim."

I look up, but I don't move.

Jim remains in his own world.

Katie leans over his bed and looks into his eyes. "I know you're in pain," she says. "I can see you are doing a good job managing it."

With this, Jim begins to talk. "The doctor told me my nerves are exposed," he says. "Like an electrical cord, with all the insulation stripped away. He says that I'll heal in time. It's plenty scary in the meantime, though."

"I know a woman who had Guillain-Barré syndrome and has recovered. Would you like me to call her and ask her to come see you? I'm sure she'd be happy to talk with you," Katie says. Jim lifts his head from the pillow. "Yes, I'd appreciate a talk with someone who's gone through this. I have so many questions." Katie says, "I'll arrange a visit in the next few days."

We walk back out into the hall. "What kind of disease is this?" Barry asks Katie.

"It's an acute inflammation of the nerves," she tells him. "You can see how painful it is; just the slightest touch can be excruciating. There may be a few random symptoms, but in the beginning it's easy to overlook them. Then suddenly the body just stops working, and it's baffling because we have no idea why. Fortunately, most patients do make a full recovery."

"Did you notice? Moritz never touched him." 🐾

Postscript

Dear Barry,

My daughter and I were the ones that were so pleased to meet you at the dog show in Missoula. Well, perhaps that narrows us down to just about EVERYBODY. We were the ones from Huson, and my daughter, Mara, told you she keeps her book about Moritz right by her bed, and we talked about the "Moritz Factor."

I am writing to tell you that meeting you and Moritz was a real high point for us. You told us it was a gift to see our faces light up when we saw you (actually, when we saw Moritz!), but I want to tell you the rest of the story. Mara's face does not light up very much these days. So seeing you and watching her reaction was a gift for me, as well.

Mara was born with generalized neuromuscular weakness and a hearing impairment. In addition to that, she was taken from her birth family and placed in foster care at one month old for reasons having to do with her birth family's problems. I met her when she was two years old, and we became adopted. On the way home, Mara and I talked about the fact that when she was so ill she didn't get a chance to meet Moritz. But she told me in the car that meeting him yesterday "made her complete." This is a big statement, and I believe it has many levels to it. After we met you she started to cry, but they were happy tears, and I believe she was able to heal just a little bit more that day.

Thank you so much for spending the time to talk with us.

Mara was taken with the fact that you were really listening to her. Because of you and Moritz, she and I were able to share a transforming moment together, and as you know, those are priceless.

As for figuring out what Moritz has, that elusive Moritz Factor, I wouldn't worry about it too much. The most magical moments in life are better left unexplained.

Best wishes,
Cory Davis

About the Author

With Moritz's arrival, Barry J. Schieber's life changed. He had to make room for a big-hearted charismatic being who exuded calmness and joy. Suddenly, many old habits disappeared and life became far more adventurous. Wanting to share some of their stories, Barry began to write. He founded Silent Moon Books in 2002 to publish some of these tales.

There are now five Moritz books. This has all been a bit surreal for Barry who, before Moritz, had never written a book. You can learn more about this unusual duo at www.silentmoonbooks.com.

About the Illustrator

Kelynn Z. Alder is an artist whose work with indigenous people has led her to travel and live in many lands and has appeared in numerous national and international publications.

In her own forthcoming book Kelynn describes her life-changing move from her New York City studio to suburban Long Island. Being six months pregnant was not enough. Her husband talked her into also including a Bernese mountain dog puppy in their nest.

The new puppy brought a balance of havoc and humor to their lives, so much so that they could not resist bringing home another Berner puppy! As the family continued to expand, Kelynn discovered a source of inspiration for painting and writing—the adventures and misadventures with her four-legged companions.

When she read *Nose to Nose* Kelynn knew she'd found a kindred spirit in Barry. So, when he and Moritz were in New Hampshire, a six-hour drive away from Long Island, Kelynn took her children out of school and drove up to meet them at their book signing.

After their meeting, Barry asked Kelynn if she would be interested in illustrating his latest collection of stories about the wondrous healing powers of Moritz. Without hesitation, she answered, "Yes!"

"This project was a gift, and painting the images from the stories was a delight," Kelynn says. For more information about the artist, travel to her website: www.kelynnalder.com.

Other Books About Mortiz

Nose to Nose: A Memoir of Healing
A Gift to Share: The Story of Moritz
An Open Heart: A Story About Moritz
A Peaceful Mind: Travels with Moritz

Please visit
www.silentmoonbooks.com
for updates, teacher information, photos
and the continuing journey.